THE

NO PLOT?
NO PROBLEM!

 Novel-Writing Kit

By Chris Baty, Founder of National Novel Writing Month

CHRONICLE BOOKS
SAN FRANCISCO

ISBN 0-8118-5483-3

DESIGN BY rise-and-shine studio
Typeset in ITC Franklin Gothic
Manufactured in China

Chronicle Books endeavors to use environmentally
responsible paper in its gift and stationery products.

Distributed in Canada by
Raincoast Books
9050 Shaughnessy Street
Vancouver, B.C. V6P 6E5

10 9 8 7 6 5 4 3 2 1

Chronicle Books LLC
85 Second Street
San Francisco, CA 94105
www.chroniclebooks.com

Make voyages! Attempt them! There's nothing else.

—Tennessee Williams

Welcome!

By opening this booklet, you've become part of something wonderful. That thing—the Great Monthlong Noveling Adventure—is a bookish joyride that will change the way you write, change the way you read, and change, a little bit, your sense of what's possible in life.

Most importantly, it can also get you out of washing any dishes for an entire month.

Sounding better and better, isn't it?

My name is Chris Baty, and I'm the founder of National Novel Writing Month. National Novel Writing Month—NaNoWriMo for short—is a 30-day kick in the pants for would-be writers, a no-holds-barred "contest," in which participants are required to write a 50,000-word (roughly 175-page) novel in November. People sign up through the organization's Web site, but there are no entry fees, judges, or prizes. What you take away from the month is the experience. And a brand-new manuscript.

When I first organized NaNoWriMo in 1999, 21 of us took the plunge. Today, more than 60,000 amateur writers take part from all corners of the globe. Participants' novels have gone on to win major national awards and land book deals from big-time publishers. For most of us, though, the event is less a path to fame or fortune as it is a chance to just spend a riotously fun, deliriously productive month bashing out a book.

To me, novel writing is also a fantastic vacation from the seriousness of adulthood, a trip back in time to that point in our lives when all we did was make stuff up. As kids, we were *all* novelist protégés. We spent our days exploring the points-of-view of spaceship captains, Bolshoi ballerinas, and mad-scientist inventors. We slipped into the skins of pirates and actresses and world-class BMX riders, turning the most meager of backyard backdrops into Oscar-worthy sets.

If we wanted to stage a concert, we did. If we wanted to make a book or paint a picture, we did that, too. We tried all sorts of things—eating cat food, jumping off roofs, constructing lung-scalding cigarettes out of notebook paper and leaves. From our experiments we built a log of experiences that shaped our lives and loves. We were ambidextrous and moving, doing, making. Or watching TV.

Dang, I watched a lot of TV.

Anyway, things have changed a little bit since then. We're still watching TV, but our identities have become more concrete. We are editorial assistants. We are environmental engineers. We are marketing managers. We are boyfriends and wives.

Our weekends are a little more directed as well. We get caught up on sleep. We see movies or go to concerts. We take our children to soccer games and birthday parties. We buy groceries and do laundry. We work though a horrid array of to-do lists.

The problem, though, is that we're so busy trying to get things done that we're not really *trying* anything. With all the resources of adulthood at our disposal—drivers' licenses, credit cards, unrestricted access to chocolate—we tend to walk the same familiar ground over and over. Somehow the broad palette with which we painted our lives 20 or 30 or 40 years ago has narrowed to a few primary colors: work, relationships, family, travel.

They're all important, to be sure. But they're not the whole picture. The whole picture is one of responsible adults *and* daredevil BMX bandits, fearsome mad scientists, and ballerinas in pink tutus. Because we're just as imaginative as we were as kids. Probably more so. That creativity doesn't just atrophy and fall away. It builds and swells. The fewer outlets we allow it, the harder it pushes to break out. Our inner spaceship captains are still there, still looking to fly. And our overlooked scribes have been constructing masterpieces while we sleep.

Which brings me to this kit.

Most novel-writing guides set out on the admirable mission of teaching people how a novel works. In these how-to tomes, authors lay out the basics of story and craft, and warn against the common missteps that could sink a novel or brand a writer as an amateur in the eyes of agents or publishers.

For all their good information, these books inevitably lack one important thing: actual novel writing. After providing a comprehensive list of the terrifying ghouls lying in wait for the unsuspecting novelist, they pat the fledgling writer on the back and close up shop, sending the writer out to face the blank page alone.

Things are different here. When you dive into your novel next month, I'll be right there beside you, cheering you on and offering advice to keep your spirits and word count high. I'll also be there to tell you to get your butt back in the writing chair when the tentacles of TV and the Internet begin tugging you away from your book.

The other big difference between this kit and other how-to books on writing is that I don't believe in ghouls or missteps. I also don't believe in great first drafts. What I believe in—and this is an idea shared by Anne Lamott, Stephen King, and other professional novelists—is the importance of completed first drafts. Making that journey from "Once upon a time" to "they lived happily ever after" (or "and the monsters devoured all of them," as the case may be) is one of the most fun and juicy adventures you'll ever undertake.

To make the most of that adventure, I'm going to ask you to write in a way that may feel a little uncomfortable at first. I want you to forget about revisions. You'll be turning off the spell-checker and abandoning the quest for pretty sentences.

It may sound like a remedial approach to writing, but in fact it's practical and results-oriented. Because revising and rewriting each paragraph of a novel until it's ready for a bookstore shelf is a surefire way to collect an incomplete collection of exquisite paragraphs.

This kit has a more epic agenda. We're going to shoot for the entire dramatic arc, for the roar of the crowd, for the ticker tape drifting down on us in slow motion as we type our final sentence, run one last word count, and then close the book on a truly triumphant month.

This is big.

This is very big.

And it's yours for the taking. But to get there, you need to give yourself permission to make messes. To write ungainly sentences and create absolutely atrocious dialogue. I know it's going to hurt to leave ugly prose in your book. It may not be the way you've written in the past. And this may not be the way you choose to write in the future (though I have a sneaky feeling you're going to end up loving it). It is, however, a fantastic path toward getting a novel written and a truly enchanting way to spend a month.

Incidentally, it's also a ticket back to the pink tutus and BMX bikes we left behind on the road to adulthood. One of the fringe benefits of writing for completion rather than perfection is that you shed decades of stressful nit-picking and self-editing—trading those tiresome creatures for a renewed sense of wonder at the sheer joy of making stuff. Next month is a chance to craft a shimmering universe of your own devising, to dream a world awake and watch the characters you invent take on lives of their own. We're not going to edit any of it as it comes out, suspending all judgment and criticism until we're through.

Quantity is in. Quality is out. The strange thing about shooting for quantity over quality, though, is that you end up getting both. You'll see more clearly what I mean once you start your book.

So without further ado, let's take a closer look at the kit and begin getting you ready for your novel.

Delving into the Kit

A stack of cards, a calendar, a mysterious envelope, a noveling affidavit, a shiny badge. While they all may look normal enough, the items sitting before you actually represent the single most powerful aggregation of scientifically calibrated, diabolically helpful novel-writing mojo ever assembled in one cardboard box.

What these tools will do, in manners both straightforward and sneaky, is help you write. Copiously. Freely. And, at various points in Weeks Two and Three, bitterly and begrudgingly. That's okay. As long as the words keep flowing. Because the absolute key in getting a first-draft of a novel written is to *keep moving forward.*

The items packed into this kit will rocket you foward with aplomb. Each of the implements is a papery dynamo built to bolster resolve, lower self-criticism, and refine your caffeine-intake strategies so that you can fly right past the hurdles that cause so many writers to give up before their book really has a chance to get going.

Along the way, we'll get a brief history of telephonic salutations and learn why killer whales are a lot like novelists. We'll hear inspiring tales of peripatetic cheesecake consumption and find out why your friends are going to be more interested in your daily writing habits than you are.

So what do we have here?

THE MIGHTY NOVEL PROGRESS LOG

Think of this calendar as your game board for a month of literary high jinks. It serves as a record of accomplishments past and a visual reminder of deeds yet to come. It's also a very visible way to register your ongoing triumphs and setbacks so your cheerleaders will know if it's time to break out in applause or break out the whips. (We'll talk more about these all-important cheerleaders later.)

Proper use: Label it with the appropriate headings, then use a crayon, colored pencil, or pen to chart your writing progress each day, as well as your overall progress for the month.

Increase its power by: Noting your "Onerosity" coupons' (*see* "Onerosity" coupons, *page 13*) due dates on the left-hand side of the progress log and dividing each writing session into 500- or 1,000-word blocks, taking a moment to color in your progress each time you cross a threshold. Also, consider making copies of the Progress Log, keeping one at home and one at work where others can see it.

Recommended Daily Allowance (RDA): Use and fill in the Log every day you write.

THE NOVELING AFFIDAVIT

This is a binding document that lays out your rights and responsibilities as a monthlong novelist. The signature line on the contract, incidentally, has been implanted with an ink-sensitive nanotechnology tool. Once signed, the contract will broadcast your novel-writing intentions throughout the troposphere, and a stream of novel-worthy characters, storylines, and settings will begin beaming into your brain (see page 24 for details).

Proper use: Read it carefully, then sign and date it. Fill in the start date and due date; then find a friend, relative, or potential novelist groupie to cosign it as your witness.

Increase its power by: Really signing it. Signing with your mind is not nearly as effective. As with the Progress Log, you can extend the usefulness of the contract through strategic placement. Plant a copy near your television, Internet-ready computer, telephone, and anywhere else you think you might seek procrastinating refuge from your noveling duties.

RDA: To be completed before writing starts.

DAILY NOVELING BRIEFS

 No, we're not talking about special writing underwear here. The briefs in question are daily pep talks and meditations designed to provide daily encouragement and insight for your noveling adventure. The briefs are intended to be read in order, from Brief 1 to Brief 31.

Proper use: On your first writing day, flip the Day 1 card over and read it. Move through the briefs one day at a time. Do not skip ahead. Skipping ahead will bring about dire medical repercussions, as your brain, overfilled with knowledge harvested before its time, may end up exploding. Unfortunately, Chronicle Books does not have the legal resources available to handle legal claims related to head-poppage during the writing process, so please refrain from reading any cards before their applicable dates.

Increase their power by: Reading a card every day, whether or not you have time to write that day.

RDA: One card per day. Remember the dreaded head-poppage!

MAGNA CARTA PAGES

 When it comes to monthlong noveling, the biggest hurdle for most writers is not the problem of finding the time, but that of finding a subject worth writing about. The Magna Carta exercises address that challenge. And for those of us who have some ideas already but worry that they may not be sufficiently book-worthy, this exercise will also create a personalized list of hazards to watch out for once the writing begins.

Proper use: Follow the instructions on pages 25–29.

Increase their power by: Keeping the Magna Carta I list close at hand during Week One. The Magna Carta II list is essential re-reading for Weeks Two and Three.

RDA: To be completed as soon as possible before writing starts.

"ONEROSITY" COUPONS

 Self-inflicted deadlines don't carry the same motivational weight as those given to us by bosses, teachers, and other people who scare us. These coupons are designed to help give your monthlong deadline some teeth, and to help keep you from falling too far behind in your daily word-count goals. The coupons also encourage friends and family to take a *very* personal interest in your daily writing habits.

Proper use: When you feel your commitment waning, ask a friend or family member to pick an onerous chore they'd like to have you do for them. Agree to perform this chore should you fail to produce a certain number of words by the agreed-upon deadline (3,000 new words by Friday, for instance). Fill out a coupon and give it to them, moving on to make a similar offer for another friend. And another. And another. Keep the receipt stub near your writing area as a reminder of just how miserable your life is going to be if you don't make your promised word-count goal.

Increase their power by: Using up most of the coupons in the first two and a half weeks. The most challenging period in the endeavor falls between words 15,000 and 30,000. I'll get into the reasons for this in Section Four, but for now just know that it's okay to use the lion's share of your coupons early on.

RDA: Whenever you feel your will weakening.

PUBLIC NOVELING MOMENTUM RE-CHARGER (PNMR) STICKERS

Over the course of a long month, it's inevitable that your enthusiasm for the project will flag. It's also inevitable that your cheering section, so excited and encouraging when you start writing, will eventually begin wondering when you'll abandon the whole thing so they can start having conversations with you about something other than your work in progress. The PNMR stickers help encourage communication about your novel with the outside world, reminding all who see it that you are undertaking something enormous and heroic.

Proper use: "Ask Me About My Novel" PNMR stickers should be applied to the novelist's person at the start of each noveling week, to be worn for at least an entire day.

Increase their power by: Using them as a bookish conversation starter around attractive strangers. The PNMR stickers are a great way for shy or self-deprecating writers to tip off cute baristas or bartenders about their sexy novelist-in-the-making status.

RDA: Once per week during the noveling month.

THE "I QUIT" ENVELOPE

 For many novelists, this is the only part of the kit that will never be used. If you find yourself completely losing the will to continue, though, and are on the verge of hanging up your keyboard and dropping out of the race, pull out the letter and read it.

Proper use: Break seal, unfold the letter inside, and read carefully.

Increase its power by: Reading it with a jumbo-size coffee in hand.

RDA: Once, only if you're on the verge of throwing yourself (or your manuscript) off a bridge. The goal is to leave the "I Quit" envelope unopened.

THE RADIANT BADGE OF THE TRIUMPHANT WORDSMITH

 This is *the* status symbol for monthlong novelists, worn by those mighty, majestic souls who cross the finish line in the allotted amount of time.

Proper use: Pin proudly and prominently onto lapel, bag, back pocket, or hat at a flattering angle after crossing over the 50,000-word finish line.

Increase its power by: Giving the badge to a trusted friend or family member before the writing starts. Inform your badge-keeper that you'll be back in one month with a 50,000-word novel in hand to reclaim your rightful medal of honor. At the pinning ceremony, demand that the badge-keeper henceforth address you as "Your Literary Highness."

RDA: To be worn at all academic ceremonies, sporting events, and family reunions for the rest of your life.

Preparing to Write

STEP ONE: PICK YOUR MONTH

When to begin? The answer, in a nutshell, is soon. As soon as you cracked open this booklet, your imagination began prepping the novel-writing workshop, sweeping out the dusty corners and sending some exploratory creative juices flowing through the piping. To take advantage of this momentum, think about heading out into the novel-writing frontier as soon as you can.

Some months, however, *are* better suited for writing a book than others. The ideal month is one in which you won't be traveling much, and when your work-, home-, or school-load isn't at a frenzied peak. Other hallmarks of good temporal climates include months blessed by five weekends, months shrouded in miserable weather, months bearing at least one three-day weekend, and months that aren't February.

STEP TWO: PICK YOUR PLAYERS

Great things of course have been done by solitary workers; but they have usually been done with double the pains they would have cost if they had been produced in more genial circumstances.

—Henry James

Novel writing is a fantastic one-player game. But it's also an ideal opportunity to spend time with friends.

For me, stumbling into novel-writing was a little like discovering that my computer monitor was actually a portal to a vast and thriving world, a metropolis of heroes and villains who had been going about their daily lives for years just an inch inside my computer screen. This was one of the true "Eureka!" moments of my life, and ever since I made that discovery, I spend as much time as possible spying on the residents of that parallel world.

As you slip into your own fictional world in the coming months, you're going to be eager to talk with someone about the weird, wonderful things you witness there. There is no better ear to bend about it than the one attached to a friend who has also been spending their evenings bathing in the CRT light of their own enchanted universe.

Tackling the novel with a friend or two does more than just give you companionship for a strange journey. It also helps ensure that you keep at it when the going gets tough. Cyclists in the Tour de France ride in tight groups called *pelotons* because traveling inside of one is much more pleasant than riding solo—the group's pace keeps you from falling behind, and peloton riders encounter 20 percent less wind resistance than those outside the pack. In the novel-writing world, when you know at least one other person is facing a month of early mornings or late nights, you're going to feel much less disgruntled about your own writing schedule. Also, the fear that your writing buddy is going to leave you in the dust, word-countwise, allows you to tap into a spirit of friendly competition that will distract you from the somewhat terrifying fact that you're both writing reasonably accomplished novels in a very short amount of time.

As you consider possible writing buddies, remember that they needn't live in your city to be a helpful force. Thanks to e-mail, instant-messaging, and cheap long-distance, writers can encourage each other (and mock each other's dwindling word counts) from half a world away. If you're interested in bringing some friends with you, consider inviting the following:

Family Members: There's no surer way to guarantee a productive month than challenging a family member to a 50,000-word write-off. Siblings, especially, would rather die than let a brother or sister show them up, making novel completion a fait accompli for both parties.

The Up-for-Anything: These are the enthusiastic souls who savor the excitement of doing new things, regardless of the activity. UFAs probably haven't done much writing, but they're up for the challenge, and their unflagging enthusiasm and congenitally low stress levels make them great companions.

The Competitor: These are die-hard, aggressive types who hate to lose at anything. Though you'd never want to face one on a basketball court, the Competitor is very useful in the monthlong noveling world as a pack-leader and pacesetter.

The Creative Yearner: The CY grew up drawing, painting, writing, and playing music. In the past few years, though, the demands of daily life have forced these dreamers to put away their art supplies. The month of ferocious noveling will be a structured opportunity for them to get their creative juices flowing again.

The Corked Writer: This is someone who used to write but stopped when something blocked the word-well. Thirty-day novels have a way of blasting right through obstructions, and the CW will come into full bloom over the course of the month. The contact high from being nearby when it happens is unforgettable.

Your Book Group: One of the great side effects of writing a novel is the deepened understanding it brings to books you read. This makes it an ideal activity for book groups. If you're in a reading group, propose that instead of tackling someone else's

Novelists to Avoid When Picking Your Team

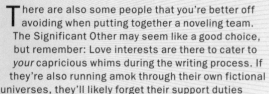

There are also some people that you're better off avoiding when putting together a noveling team. The Significant Other may seem like a good choice, but remember: Love interests are there to cater to *your* capricious whims during the writing process. If they're also running amok through their own fictional universes, they'll likely forget their support duties and believe that they, too, deserve attention, treats, and backrubs on demand. No siree. Also to be avoided:

- **The Busybody** eagerly commits to a million things but ends up canceling at the last minute.

- **The Albatross** has been working unhappily on the same manuscript for umpteen years, limping under the psychic weight of the unfinished project. If Albatrosses can set their old book aside for a month and start anew, they'll do great. But if they insist on using the 30-day push to try and finish the old book, they're going to be miserable. Which will make you miserable, too.

- **The Marketing Maniac** is someone who has spent time in or near the publishing industry and has come to measure a book's worth by its sales potential. These types have a deep understanding of the fiction-writing market but they'll discard many of their best ideas—and discourage yours—because they don't sound marketable enough.

book next month, you each write your own. Then meet every week during the month to commiserate and celebrate your progress. When it's over, each member can bring a copy of his or her favorite passage to share.

STEP THREE: SPREAD THE WORD

I once believed successful novel writing required authors remove themselves to a tower, garret, or gable, where, after a period of stoic gestation, they would emerge, soot-stained and wild-haired, with novels in hand.

It didn't take long for me to see that my ideas about the value of writerly retreat had been a little off base. Making the novel a matter of private toil, in fact, only reduces the chances that you'll actually get a book finished. Because it shuts out one of the most important forces in the history of the creative world. I'm talking, of course, about the fear of public embarrassment.

In the same way that a group working toward the same goal creates an unstoppable momentum, so will the hopes, expectations, and interest of an attentive audience keep your body going when your mind is ready to quit.

Your noveling cheerleaders are there to bug you about your word count. They'll celebrate with you when you're ahead and make you feel like a loser when you're behind. And you can never have too many of them, so when you set out to tackle the wild, woolly challenge of novel writing, you should let *everyone* know what you're up to.

To help line up your cheerleaders, send out an e-mail or make a few phone calls before the month begins, and encourage all your loved ones to check in on your word count anytime they talk to you. (This is also a good time to let them know that they can't read the thing until you're done.) And be sure they have your mailing address handy for massive shipments of chocolate-covered espresso beans, super-absorbent sweatbands, high-energy CD mixes, and other noveling accessories.

Don't worry: Most of the time, you won't need their encouragement and won't notice their nagging. But there will be a handful of moments when your fear of looking like a quitter in front of your cute coworker or encouraging spouse will be the only thing keeping you in the game.

So start putting out the word now. You'll be very glad you did.

STEP FOUR: FILL OUT THE AFFIDAVIT

This is the last step before we begin talking about your book. Grab the most official-looking pen you can find, grab a friendly witness, and throw some dramatic, swelling music on the stereo. (I recommend the *Chariots of Fire* theme.) Make the event official by inking in a start and end date, and, finally, your signature and that of your witness.

Then put on a pot of coffee. It's time to talk novel.

STEP FIVE: THINK ABOUT YOUR BOOK

Different writers will tell you different things about how much planning and plotting you should put into your book. I happen to savor the feelings of discovery that come with moving for-

Burning the Midnight Altoid

Between work, school, family, and errands, the only time many of us have to get writing done are the quiet, pre-bed hours. Writers in their teens or 20s will have no trouble handling an occasional regimen of burning the candle at both ends. For us older writers, though, all-nighters are out of the question, and we'll need all the help we can get to keep from ruining the romantic late-night writing tableau by falling asleep at the keyboard.

Happily, there are a host of tricks you can use to turn the barren wastelands of exhausted evenings into productive writing oases. As you might expect, coffee drinkers do very well in the monthlong noveling arena, and java junkies will likely find themselves brewing up thick pots of the stuff at all hours. Green teas, along with the South American herb yerba mate, also make great coffee substitutes for those who don't like coffee's flavor. For those unfortunate souls who become jittery zombies when dosed with caffeine, there are a host of equally powerful stimulants to make the brain sparkle, even in the wee hours. Some of the best stimulants:

ward without a compass, allowing the book's direction to shift as new situations arise. I tend to start with a vague image—a small town experiencing religious visions of Walter Mondale, for instance—and then I go hide in the bushes outside my characters' homes and see what else is going on in their lives.

That said, there's no "right" approach to novel writing or pre-writing. For some left-brained types, diving into a book without any sort of plan is like water-skiing blindfolded—more of a nightmare than a thrill ride. Even if they know that their book's course will be altered somewhat during the writing process, these novelists need to have *some* outline in place before they begin. For them, spontaneity is actually enhanced by having a predetermined structure upon which they can hang fresh ideas and inspirations.

FRESH AIR: Crack a window, or, better still, go sit outside on the front steps for a few minutes. This is especially reviving if you're noveling in winter months. Plant lovers can drag all of their little friends into their writing room to create a low-intensity oxygen bar.

PEPPERMINTS: A recent NASA-funded study showed that the oils of the peppermint plant increased alertness by 30 percent and decreased fatigue by 15 percent. Peppermint tea, peppermint candies, and peppermint oil all work fine.

SPICY FOODS: These work in essentially the same way as a whiff of peppermint, giving your tri-geminal nerve a reviving jolt. Can anyone say "chips and salsa"?

SUNLIGHT: This one takes a little planning, as sunlight tends to be relatively hard to come by at 11 P.M. The good news is that sunlight absorbed during the day—even on cloudy days—has been shown to elevate moods long after the sun goes down.

WATER: If you've been feeling exhausted and cranky lately, it may be more than just a lack of sleep. Dehydration deepens feelings of fatigue. Keep a head-sized jug of the stuff close at hand while you write.

Inspiring Tales of High-Speed Mayhem

Caffeine and literature have long enjoyed a very productive relationship. Some high-speed books you might have read include Anne Rice's *Interview with a Vampire* (five weeks, for a contest deadline), William Faulkner's *As I Lay Dying* (six weeks), Robert Louis Stevenson's *The Strange Case of Dr. Jekyll and Mr. Hyde* (three days), Chuck Palahniuk's *Fight Club* (two weeks), and the first book in the Perry Mason series, which creator Erle Stanley Gardner dictated in just four days (while working half-days at his law practice no less!)

Ultimately, both approaches are great, and you probably know right now whether you fall into the "let's carefully map out major plot points" or the "let's wing it and see what happens!" camp. Either way, I recommend giving yourself a limited amount of time to plan your book. Past a certain point, researching and outlining are just ways to avoid actually writing. The bad news is that you're *never* going to feel adequately prepared to start your novel. The good news is that the problems you anticipate in your plot or characters will resolve themselves in unexpected ways as you move through the book.

Another welcome bonus you'll receive along the way is an unbelievable surplus of real-life material. The universe absolutely loves amateur novelists, and it will be sending you all manner of intriguing characters, juicy plot points, and novel-ready dialogue via passers-by, newspapers, and television in the coming weeks. Pick up a small notebook from the office supply or stationery store, and get in the habit of locking in your thoughts and inspirations as they arrive.

THE MAGNA CARTA EXERCISES

The universe can't be counted on to do *all* the work, though. To help you figure out some of the people, places, and things that should have starring roles in your book, I recommend taking a few minutes to fill out the two Magna Carta pages that follow. This is an exercise borrowed from *No Plot? No Problem!* and it will help refine your ideas about your novel and provide you a list of items to consider (or avoid) while writing your book.

Your assignment is to brainstorm all the elements you love in novels. Be as specific or broad as you like, and write each one down on the card as they occur to you.

My list, to help give you some ideas, looks like this:

MAGNA CARTA I

First-person narration

Books where the city becomes a character in the story

Quirky characters

True love

Found objects

Disappointment

Music

Catharsis

Feisty old people

Modern settings

Strong, charismatic protagonists

A little guy triumphing over a bully

Improbable romances

Smart but unpretentious writing

Urban settings

Cliffhanger chapter endings

Characters who are at turning points in their lives

Books set in the workplace

Happy endings

Okay, go ahead and fill up your list.

MAGNA CARTA I

Why did we just do this? Because the things that you appreciate as a reader are also the things you'll likely excel at as a writer. These bits of language, color, and technique, for whatever reason, make sense to your creative brain. These are the Elements You Understand. As you point your skis down the slopes of your monthlong novel, you'll do well to try and navigate a path that takes you through as many of these juicy elements as possible.

You'll likely be adding more elements to the Magna Carta I (MCI) list over the coming week, but for now, let's move on to the second Magna Carta list. For the MCII, jot down everything that bores, exhausts, or depresses you in novels. Again, feel free to be as specific or wide-ranging as you like.

Mine would include:

MAGNA CARTA II

Irredeemably malicious main characters

Books set on farms

Books that employ too much math or science

Mentally ill main characters

Food or eating as a central theme

Books that require a genealogy chart on the inside cover to remember who's who

Ghosts, monsters, or demons

Dysfunctional sibling dramas

Books consisting largely of a character's thoughts

Weighty moral themes

Books set in the nineteenth century

Unhappy endings

Fill out your MCII.

MAGNA CARTA II

As you spend your next week thinking about what you want to have in your novel, keep the MCII close at hand, so you'll remember what *not* to put in your story. I know it seems silly to remind yourself to keep things you dislike out of your novel, but be warned: The entries on your MCII are vicious, cunning little buggers, and given the slightest opening, they will find their way into your book.

The reason they'll make their way onto your pages is related to the same principle of self-betterment that causes us to bring high-brow tomes home from the bookstore, knowing full well they'll go straight onto the bookshelf and never be touched again. (My latest of these is a slim volume detailing, of all things, the natural history of dust.)

We buy these books because we feel that they are in some way good for us. It's the literature-as-bran-flake philosophy: If something is dry and unpalatable, it must be doing something good to our constitutions. This thinking also carries over into the writing realm. If we're worried that our story is lacking substance, the first thing most of us will automatically reach for are the bran morsels from our MCII.

The other reason we allow book-ruining MCII elements into our stories is because many of us are saddled with the pernicious belief that we find certain subjects boring or exhausting because we're not smart enough to be engaged by them.

This is all total nonsense. As you work through your novel, keep this in mind: If you won't enjoy reading it, you won't enjoy writing it. Your novel is not a self-improvement campaign. Your novel is a jubilant hoedown set to your favorite music, a 30-day visit to a candy store where everything is free and nothing is fattening. When you're wondering what to write about, always grab the guilty pleasures over the bran flakes. Write your joy, and good things will follow.

At the Starting Blocks

Before we turn on the computer or open the notebook and send those first lines racing across the page, let's do a quick review.

The Goal: The goal is to write a 50,000-word novel from scratch in a calendar month. Writing begins as 12:00:00 A.M. on the first day of the chosen month, and ends at 11:59:59 P.M. on the month's final day.

The Winner: Anyone who has written 50,000 words or more wins. Depending on the number of people writing alongside you, there might be many winners. Or there might just be you.

The Prize: Winners shall receive a first draft of a surprisingly competent novel, a marked increase in their creative confidence, and a curious desire to write another novel soon. Winners will also get to wear the hallowed Radiant Badge of the Triumphant Wordsmith every day of their lives until it falls apart.

What you need to play: About 12 hours of writing time each week. A word-processing device (pen and paper, computers, etc.). This kit.

TEN VERY IMPORTANT RULES TO KEEP IN MIND DURING YOUR WRITING MONTH

 There are no *can'ts* in the world of monthlong novel writing. You *can* do it, and you can do it with panache. Tens of thousands of people complete monthlong novels every year, many of whom are afflicted by full-time jobs, grumpy significant others, and demanding children. No matter your schedule or level of writing expertise, you can tackle this challenge and triumph. Begin the game knowing that you will go the distance, and you're already halfway there.

 You don't have to write a *good* novel. Ol' Papa Hemingway, not known for mincing words, said: "The first draft of anything is shit," and he's right. No matter how long you give yourself to write a first draft, it's going to need work later. *Everyone's* first drafts do, and, happily, the revision process is its own engaging adventure. So don't worry about getting it perfect on the first go-round.

 With this in mind, all words are good words. This is a very different kind of writing from the one we learned in school. In the realm of the 30-day novel you must write recklessly and fearlessly, try weird things and follow questionable tangents just to see where they lead. Be quick and audacious, and view the month as an experiment in pure output, one in which you focus on building without tearing down. Apart from a few sentences here and there, you should try to delete nothing—all of it may prove useful at some point, and every preposition and modifier moves you one tick closer to meeting the 50,000-word goal.

 Rewards, treats, and self-praise are mandatory. Professional writers get money for putting themselves through this ordeal. In lieu of wages, you are required to deluge yourself with nonstop pampering. Indulge your whims for take-out Thai, Swiss chocolates, inspirational novels, CDs, and expensive spa treatments. When you make a big push and meet your word-count goal, reward yourself with something you've always wanted but never felt you truly deserved. You're writing a novel in a month, for pete's sake. You deserve it.

 The novel you write must be a completely new venture. Meaning you are not allowed to spend the month tacking on 50,000 words to a story you've already started. As counterintuitive as it seems, extending an old novel by 50,000 words is much more difficult than writing a new one from scratch. You just have too much invested in its outcome, and you will agonize over each sentence. That said, you're welcome to research and plan your new novel to your heart's content before starting. Character sketches, plot points, and outlines are all A-OK. Just no previously written prose.

 Shameless acts of word padding (characters reciting *The Canterbury Tales* in their sleep, avoidance of contractions, protracted singing of "Row, Row, Row Your Boat," etc.) are acceptable and encouraged. Employment of such devices, however, must be declared to any fellow novelists at the time of their use.

 You are allowed to borrow liberally from your life and the lives of those around you and still call it fiction. Professional novelists do this all the time, even if they don't always admit it. In fact, writing a heavily autobiographical novel is a great idea, especially if this is your first book. Just remember to change the names before you let your mother read it.

Sharing lengthy excerpts from your work in progress is forbidden until the month's close. The impulse to share your novel with those around you is going to be irresistible at times, especially when characters become more willful and plot breakthroughs come fast and furious. But sharing is rarely as satisfying as you would hope, and it often ends up dampening your enthusiasm when your audience doesn't react as you'd hoped. Wait and dazzle your loved ones when the entire draft is finished.

 No sharing novel-writing duties. The responsibility and satisfaction of writing a 50,000-word novel is yours and yours alone.

 Novelists are not allowed to do dishes during the month, theirs or anyone else's. Cleaning of bath- rooms and acts of mopping are similarly forbidden. The same goes for returning phone calls you don't want to return, and running errands for friends and family members. It's simply too risky for your hands. Sorry.

Writing!

The day before you start your book, do a final run-though. Do you have your notebook to jot down writing ideas? Is the affidavit signed and the Progress Log hung? Does at least one other person know you're about to set out into Novel Land? Is your cheerleader currently making you a five-course going-away dinner and sobbing at the thought of so much bravery and literary derring-do amassed in a single human being?

Okay. Three out of four isn't bad. If you're feeling a little panicked, it's okay. Everything will fall into place once you begin.

In addition to the daily writing briefs, I've put together an overview of each week for you, complete with an assigned reading, a word-count bare minimum you need to meet, a few extra-credit assignments, and an FAQ pertaining to that week's challenge.

Now, put down the booklet, come back to this page on your first noveling morning, and we'll run through the week ahead.

WEEK ONE

What is writing a novel like?
The beginning: A ride through a spring wood.
The middle: The Gobi desert.
The end: Going down the Cresta run.

—Edith Wharton

Assignment: Read the first seven Daily Noveling Briefs (at a rate of one per day). Fight your temptation to read ahead (see cranium exploding, earlier). Close each writing session with some shading time on your Progress Log. Do not color outside the lines. Just kidding. Color all over the place.

Word Count Minimum: You'll need to put away 11,669 words by the close of the first week or risk feeling overwhelmed at the start of Week Two.

Extra Credit:

1) On your first writing weekend, stockpile a few thousand words above your writing quota. Think of this surplus as a free savings account you've just opened in the Greater Word Bank of Novel Land. Draw from this account at your leisure, adding back to it on good days and borrowing against it on the nights when turning off the computer and going to bed early is the only thing that will salvage your sanity. *Note:* In Week One, making deposits will be much, much easier than it will be in coming weeks.

2) Using Blogger, LiveJournal, or any other free online diary site, set up a blog that will chart the meteoric rise of your novelist stature during your writing month. Include (very short) bits of your novel if you like, along with each day's word count totals. Be sure also to fill it with plausible yet greatly exaggerated tales of your literary accomplishments. Discuss any bears you've wrestled and your latest victories or defeats at the hands of the ever-present procrastination demons. Decorate it with pictures of you staring pensively at your screen. Then send a link for the blog out to your cheerleaders. Be sure to tell them that your blog has a way of telling you who has visited every day, and make it clear that those who don't visit and leave encouraging comments on a regular basis will later be removed from your will.

Week One FAQ

How do I start? Do I really just sit down and start writing?
You bet!

This is going suspiciously well. Should I be worried?
Do you remember making posters for lemonade stands or
backyard plays as a kid? The first couple of letters you drew on
the poster always came out great—they were all the same size
and looked pretty much like the letters they were supposed to.
And then you tried to make an S and it sort of looked like a col-
lapsed nematode, and your K looked like a narcoleptic H. And
then you realized you were about to hit the edge of your poster
but you still had three more letters left in whatever word you
were writing? Week One is like the first couple letters drawn
on a childhood poster. It's awesome. You're just throwing out
scenes and introducing people without really having to connect
them in any way.

Enjoy this moment. It's a sweet dose of pure creativity. The
nematode will appear in Week Two. But by then, you will be a
mighty novelist, and will have no trouble defeating it.

**What's the optimal way to rack up my daily allotment of
words? Should I be sticking to some sort of regimen?**
A lot of people with full-time jobs get up an hour earlier than
usual, and then bolster their word counts from morning writing sessions with a few evening and weekend efforts. Other
people write their entire novels while commuting on public
transportation, or sneak in a few hours while they should be
working. Whether or not you have a laptop will likely determine
your work habits, but whatever your technology situation, the
ideal approach is to try out a variety of strategies in Week
One. You'll discover one that has you writing when you feel
most alert and awake—that's the regimen to stick with.

 DO NOT READ ONWARD UNTIL WEEK TWO.

WEEK TWO

Assignment: Daily Writing Briefs 8–14. Keep an eye on your MCI list for plot ideas as you cast about for things your characters can do. Complete the "Unbearable Lightness of Being Less Available Exercise" (see next page). Start handing out "Onerosity" coupons like a maniac. Be sure to update your Progress Log after each session.

Word Count Minimum: Make it to 20,000 words. This is 3,000 words behind pace, but, hey, this is a tough week. Also: If you make it through Week Two on pace or above it, you are in the top 5 percent of monthlong novelists everywhere, and you deserve a huge reward. Maybe a new MP3 player? Or maybe a new outfit? Something good.

Extra Credit:

1) Write every day during Week Two, even if you can only get in a few hundred words each session. Characters are sort of like dogs; they tend to start tearing up bedding and peeing on things when they don't get enough attention. Keep your slippers in good shape by dropping by your fictional world every single day during Week Two. This is also a great idea because your connection to your book is going to be at its most tenuous over the next seven days. Of the large number of people who abandon their novels in NaNoWriMo, most do it in Week Two. Those who are still writing when the sun rises on Week Three are almost always those who end up crossing the finish line.

2) Do a search on blog index Technorati.com and see if anyone else out there in the blogosphere is taking part in a monthlong writing challenge (chances are good you'll find someone). If you find others who 1) are not ax-murderers, and 2) seem to be going through the same things you are, shoot them an e-mail, and let them know they're not alone. *Note:* E-mail exchanges with other novelists do not count toward your overall word count. Even if they're very creative.

The Unbearable Lightness of Being Less Available Exercise

Now that you've been working on your novel for a full seven days, it's time to do an exercise designed to help you free up more writing time in the midst of your hectic life. In the left column, make a list of the top three negotiable activities that have the most impact on the amount of time you're spending on your writing. "Negotiable" refers to things over which you have some say as to when and how they get done. Childcare could be negotiable, because you could hire a sitter or call in a favor with a family member or friend for a limited amount of time. Going to your full-time job, however, is *non*-negotiable, because hiring a babysitter to take your place there would likely result in you earning the displeasure of your boss.

Go ahead and make the list. Then, brainstorm a second list in the right-hand column—lay out the changes you can make to mitigate the effect of these forces in the coming week to give yourself more time to write. Get creative, and don't be afraid to call in favors. And remember, we're not talking forever here. This regimen lasts only for the next three weeks.

Here's an example of something I might put in these columns:

Internet surfing and e-mailing

This week I will:

- Only let myself check my e-mail once in the morning and once before going to bed, and the latter only if I've made my word count for the day.

- Warn friends that I'll be slow to return e-mail for the next three weeks.

- Give myself one five-minute Internet surfing break for every hour I spend writing.

Week Two FAQ

It's Day 12. Why does it feel like a truck just ran over my face? Welcome to Week Two, my friend. You've hit the challenging, inevitable juncture in your novel where all the characters you threw into the mix in Week One have to get out there and *do* something. This requires that you make a few difficult decisions. Unfortunately, this is also the point when the exhilaration of Week One wears off, and you will come to terms with the fact that this thing is going to continue for another three weeks. There's a natural energy dip, but don't worry: It will all come back in Week Three.

I'm having trouble with the whole "all words are good words" thing. My inner editor won't leave me alone, and I'm not making as much progress as I should be because I find myself editing what I wrote the day before. What can I do? First off, I'd recommend reading only the last paragraph from the previous day when you sit down at a new session. Reading everything you've written will yank you out of your creative mindset and put you into a miserable Editor Mind. The EM will be very useful once you're done with the book, but right now it's only going to prevent you from moving onward into the next segment of your book.

Try putting any prose you want to delete in italics, rather than cutting it outright. Italicizing a passage is sort of like shrink-wrapping it—it's still there to be inventoried by the word-count machine, but it's been safely cordoned off from the rest of your book and flagged for disposal when the editing begins next month.

You keep talking about the difficulties of Week Two, but it's almost the end of the week and things are still going suspiciously well for me. Am I doing something wrong? About 10 percent of writers eat this monthlong challenge for breakfast from the get-go, racking up huge word counts early and continuing their reign from there. If you make it through Week Two completely undaunted and on track, you are likely one of those blessedly wordy folks. Keep on trucking toward the finish line! The rest of us will catch up with you in a couple of weeks.

 DO NOT READ ONWARD UNTIL WEEK THREE.

WEEK THREE

Assignment: Daily Writing Briefs 15–21 on their appropriate days. Give your MCII list the hairy eyeball and make sure nothing on it is trying to worm its way into your book. Keep doling out those "Onerosity" coupons.

Word Count Minimum: Make it to 35,000 words (2,000 words behind pace).

Extra Credit:

1) End Week Three as close to 40,000 words as possible. FYI: Once you break the 39,999 mark, the course tilts sharply downward, and you'll write with a speed and agility you haven't known since Week One. From 40K, life is butter.

2) Increase the pressure on yourself by sending out invitations to a handful of friends or family for a casual get-together to celebrate your successful novel completion and return to normal life. Plan the event for the first day after this current month ends and promise them that they'll be able to gawk at a printout of your book at the party.

Week Three FAQ

My characters are starting to want to do things I don't want them to do. Way to go! You've achieved character liftoff. This happens at some point in every book. It's a little creepy at first, but it's ultimately one of the coolest aspects of novel writing. Let them have their way—if they end up doing something stupid, you can always reassert your will in the editing phase.

My cheerleaders aren't so cheerful anymore.
They just miss you. And are probably tired of your whining. Reassure them it will be over soon, but stand firm on your demands for treats and presents.

I am really far behind.
That's okay! Come-from-behind victories are a long and honored tradition in the world of monthlong noveling. Just make a point of writing above quota every day from here till close and you'll be fine.

No, I mean, I'm *really* far behind.
Like 10,000 words behind?

Uh-huh.
Okay, it's time for a Nuclear Weekend. These are much less painful than the name implies and are a great way to get your noveling groove back. This Saturday and Sunday, beg, borrow, or steal enough time to fit in a morning, afternoon, and evening session. In each session, go 40 minutes on and 20 minutes off until you hit 1,500 words. Then go do something fun. Each day, you'll rocket forward by 4,500 words, ending the weekend 9,000 words richer than you started it.

 DO NOT READ ONWARD UNTIL THE FINAL WEEK.

THE FINAL WEEK

Assignment: Daily Writing Briefs 22 through to the end of the deck, one per day. Don the Radiant Badge of the Triumphant Wordsmith.

Word Count Minimum: Make it to 50,000 words.

Extra Credit:

If you finish with a day or two to spare, try to push on past the 50,000-word point. The more you write, the more of your italics-wrapped passages (*see* Week Two, *earlier*) you can delete.

Final Week FAQ

I'm on track as far as word count, but I'm very far away from the end of the story. That's totally understandable. In its final, edited form, your book will likely be much longer than 50,000 words. But creating a complete story arc for your book now will make revision much easier later. If you're still miles away from The End with just a few days left to go, feel free to skip or abbreviate intermediary chapters, and instead write through to the conclusion of the book.

Can I have aliens come down and eat my characters?
It's your novel—you can do anything you want. If you're not so into aliens, wormholes are also a convenient option. As are tigers, for that matter.

This has been so much fun. I don't want it to end.
It won't! You can move on to revising the book you've written this month, or you can set it aside and start a new book right away. Now that you've discovered how doable novel writing can be, you can write as many books as you like, experimenting with genre, narration styles, subject matter, and other delights. Novel writing is a lifetime sport, and a world of new discoveries awaits.

ABOUT CHRIS BATY

Chris Baty is a writing cheerleader who founded National Novel Writing Month in 1999. Since then, the November writing escapade has grown to include 60,000 participants from all over the world. He has written seven distinctly unhorrible novels. His quest for the perfect cup of coffee is never-ending, and will likely kill him some day.

Thank You

Thanks to Lynda Barry, Rob Couteau, Chronicle Books, Erica Donnis, Arielle Eckstut, Katherine Fausset and the Watkins/Loomis Agency, Film Four LTD, Cynthia Foster, Danella Hocevar, Ron Hussey, Leslie Jonath, Elly Karl, Bruce Mau, Michael Morris, New Directions Publishing, Tom Parker, Peet's coffee (Sumatra blend), Michele Posner, Erin Thacker, Kevin Toyama, Gerard Van der Leun, Robert J. Williams, and the awesome folks who participate in National Novel Writing Month every year.